G & T

Oakley Flanagan

Out-Spoken Press
London

Published by Out-Spoken Press,
PO Box 78744
London, N11 9FG

A CIP record for this title is available from the British Library.

First edition published 2023
ISBN: 978-1-7399021-9-3

Typeset in Adobe Caslon
Design by Patricia Ferguson
Printed and bound by Print Resources

Out-Spoken Press is supported using public funding by the National
Lottery through Arts Council England.

Supported using public funding by

**ARTS COUNCIL
ENGLAND**

G &T

Contents

Last night I drank too much

cleaning fluid with a man
    I didn't know. The name of
    the sex,

        his username

                                for nine days

the tenth day

I came to
in the room for living I cruised

    self-conscious
    images of the plague dead
    reproduced in exacting detail

        Swallowed backdrip

The night before I attended a party at which I was to be the guest of honour, I had been considering writing a late and hurried essay on the last definitively naturalistic drama by a playwright whose main theme was desire. The drama's title derived from the elm trees of its playworld, under which the desires of its main characters manifest. A tightly plotted interplay between sparring masculine and feminine forces (the competing symbols of feminised elm trees and a monolithic stone wall) did most of the symbolic work in communicating the play's treatment of patriarchy and desire. The twin symbols were honest in that they genuinely reflected the play's configuration of female desire and male will and that made them comforting; they retained faith in a world where things really were what they seemed. I intended to make a point of linking it to an expressionist drama in which a bank cashier, living in a society that sees love in solely economic terms, steals a large sum of money with which to live out a life of sensuous excess. The bank cashier's journey to damnation is harried only once, when, walking home to the family he will later abandon, he stops at a tree in a snowfield. The tree changes instantly before his eyes into a skull, a clear sign of his spiritual death should he continue on his path. When the man arrives home however, recounting the story of the tree to his family, he fatally misreads the sign in his telling of it, claiming it as Revelation and using it to justify his pursuit of pleasures of the flesh, as if the skull were a personal vindication. I'd wanted to stress that what we think we know to be meaningful is always mediated by perspective.

Like Maps, our destination is calculated in relation to where our current location is set. But then the notification went off, alerting me to the fact of the man at my front door, so I did not write this but instead chose to go downstairs to let him in, grinning as he flicked his resealable bag like a bell.

The blown-out day begins as it ends in liquids.

His username was Voyeur, and I came to know him as one. I went downstairs to let him in, reminding him to be quiet as we made our way up the stairs. I locked the door as he fixed us a glass of water, depositing a small holdall on my bed from which he took out various outfits. Outfits he presumably carried with him on the off chance he might find a receptive model and which he used to take me through various tropes of boyhood; that I changed into and out of accordingly so that various scenarios could unfold between us. Scenarios that could never be actualised, he said, as if on account of a taboo. The current outfit I'd changed into, for example, represented a particular kind of fantasy to him; one that operated precisely not through touch but by the mere transgression of imagination. We argued about the issue until he gestured to the water and told me to listen. He explained that as a child he had been at the mercy of his father's violent temper which had marked him for life. When he grew up and came to terms with his sexuality he had cultivated an ingenious persona to sublimate the violent impulses he'd inherited through the assumption of a voyeuristic sexual identity, one that enabled him to play out sexual fantasies in which he was an active bystander. It was this erotic identity, being both dominant (in that he had full control over the subject matter) and passive (he never broke the fourth wall between the action and his status as spectator), that allowed him to become a witness to events, affording him a level of control that affirmed his sense of his own autonomy. In the company of consenting adults it meant that no real violence ensued: it was merely symbolic. He stressed that his position in such matters was more pedagogic than it was strictly penetrative, therefore it was unproblematic. He had taken his father's rage and eroticised it, beating him once and for all. I thought about his mother and where that left her. Besides, he continued, I obviously wasn't a child anymore. It was only after he said this, after I demanded he fuck me as a boy and he refused, and not when he told me he worked at a local primary school, that I knew he was a pervert. I broke the contract we had established, staring directly at him instead of pretending (as I should have) to shower oblivious to his presence, fondling himself on my bed. He'd looked away upset and when I asked if I really wasn't allowed to look at him, he reiterated the importance of staying in character in order to preserve the integrity of the scene; the essential strictures of the boundaries between us that had been agreed upon prior, him on one side of the room, me on the other.

It's about suspending your disbelief, he said.

I know, I've done this before, I said:

Fantabulosa!

for any proximate body
for one night only
for nights into days
days into weeks
for months
missed calls
a broken screen

When we arrived at the bus stop, the ageing male bachelor suddenly stepped back, stretching out his arm performatively. A gift bag rested on his forefinger, swaying like a pendulum quickly losing momentum. He placed the bag on the pavement and stepped further back with his finger still drawn. I'd anticipated he was going to drop the cord onto my finger, which by now was also extended. We were casting frozen, accusatory gestures at one another, like mimes. I bent down, withdrawing a blue silk dressing gown.

My boy in blue, he said, closing the gap between us.

He produced another cocktail cigarette and placed it between my lips. I rested it on top of the dressing gown I'd replaced inside the gift bag, telling him I'd save it for later. He didn't press me to stay another night, asking instead to show me something before I'd be gone. He thrust his hand inside the bag, withdrawing a book from beneath the hastily folded silk. The cover had been torn and the spine was so faded that, bar his introduction, it could have been anyone's biography contained within the book's dog-eared pages, prefaced by the inscription he had made by hand. 'To my lovely boy, Always…' between which, the space he'd left blank, filled by printed text.

His 'always' was a mark of restitution to preserve me on his own terms, in an effort that he might repossess me, if not in reality, then in the pages of the biography at least. He said the book told the life story of an actor whom he greatly admired, and whose rise from humble beginnings he knew by heart. He began to recount the actor's backstory as the bus made its circuitous route to our side of the road. The actor had battled against adversity and won against all the odds. I had heard this story before. He described how early on in life the boy had been recognised for his precocious talent by a benevolent father figure (who the biography attributed to, and he stressed was): a wealthy bachelor. Despite being many years his senior, the man took him in as if he were his own son and had designs on the boy to adopt him. Being below the legal age to be recognised as the boy's guardian however, the actor changed his surname in honour of the man, or so the story went. It was this man we had to thank for the creation of the star we knew today. I thanked him, telling him I'd think of him when I read it. I replaced it inside the gift bag and kissed him on the cheek, pulling away as the bus arrived. I was embarrassed to be seen with him, even by strangers I'd never see again. Embarrassed by his fur coat, his furtive gestures, his vampiric manners.

Thank you for tonight, I said. When I grow up, I want to be just like you, waving from my side of the pane as he receded into the shadows and laughing on the empty top deck, laughing, like I'd won.

I came to
in smoking areas
getting raucous
finessing strangers
I am too in the earth
& the shit

I must sing I Marilyn

into the bruised beef

Campari pores
from my slutty finger, wet
from the knife's serrated edging.

Tonight, I'm a power dress.

Happy Student Finance Day!

Red-lipped.
Cash-slicked.
Flush, thus

I'm spender
& spent — a double

as a kid twink
I was a diamond
thief. I worked
internationally
for white
collared men
well-versed
in our profession
its sanctities of hide
& seek. Older
I got visible
hawked barely legal
intimacies beneath

hairy bass, fuzzy bouncers
            I shamed men like home
        testing-kits, insisting
        my dead left
                    when the sick sun rose
                    bald as the mandates
                    when I go with a complex
                    bachelor quickly I graduate
                    to stronger drinks

this time boys it's coming up lotus my body
awakening to the full
possibilities of its erasure my absent thigh gap
leg measurements I must send
before he agrees to meet passing comment
on the thickness of my physique & general
looseness he slips right in as the room fills up

deep in my feelings
salve for the wound
a putative safety as
I drift off to roam

the pictures & pixels
go on without end in
the mauve room of
my dreams beyond
the limits of this
dimensional bed this
heavily   curtained
room I am not here
unsexed as I am my
every breath orgasm
ask how it feels I'll
tell you it's heaven
my other body be-
neath me I float on
up one giant nerve
ending   resounding
symphony so this is
love so this is love so
this is love unloosen
my ropes I want to
go higher let me
at least keep my
beautiful flower

it is as easy as lying it is as easy as lying

after[1]

---

[1] the left alive shamble   home to bed
quiet   vows to delete   the app as t
races of men   scat   t   er
ing   insurmountable as evidence
would be stigmata   accounts
whispered of   unattested to
in orderly courts of law

the flowers are everywhere
all over my jabbering hands
reciting effacement
almost entirely nameless
a man I have only just met
looking very disappointed
he says open up or leave
wash your hands & they
will still be there the flowers
give me the ocular proof
underneath our fingernails
on the ceiling of our mouths
they do not care if we live
the so very blasé flowers
our wedding-funerary meats
they take root under the sole
of my left shoe bad medicine
Spring now & I must clean
myself & property back to front

for anybody please
make me feel something

after

men wash their hands of me in the river the judge the
policeman the doctor man the insistent director with
nonbinary pronouns the straight men who own the gay sex
app the pseudo psychiatrist who had me all day as I watched
the red light become a more violent shade of red he led me
on all fours to his office offering me a session on his non-
symbolic couch I spoke at length about my childhood he
proffered PrEP I swallowed a happy baby hours passed me a
top-up seven missed calls from the mother I pray never reads
this family I cast off like unbranded clothes sporting only
Calvins a glass of water in my hand I have never been cleaner
passed through smoke & doused in fluids as one might a
pendulum before divining on a life juncture

before

I look back & wonder how I couldn't see what was to
come, staring me in the face

> I do
> as every one of us
> in this annihilated perspective
> does, convinced —

> one time, just for kicks.

How it began was like this: *Fantabulosa!*

Appreciations

Thank you to my ancestors. Thank you to my sister. Thank you to my parents. My sincere gratitude and appreciation to Queen. Thank you to Wayne Holloway-Smith and to Out-Spoken. Special thanks to Professor Charlotte Scott. Thank you to Anastasia and Courtney. Special thanks to Rachel Long and Richard Scott. Thank you to Masha Kevinovna and OPIA Collective. Special thanks to Salena Godden, thanks for everything mamma. Thank you to Apples and Snakes. Thank you to Zena Edwards, Sabrina Mahfouz and Joelle Taylor. Special thanks to Nathalie Teitler. Deepest thanks and gratitude to Bridget Minamore and Cecilia Knapp, thank you also to Roundhouse Poetry Collective. Thanks to London Library Emerging Writers Programme, and to Claire Berliner. Thank you to Genesis Jewish Book Week Emerging Writers' Programme, and to Sarah Fairbairn. Thank you to Southbank Centre's New Poets Collective, and to Will Harris, Vanessa Kisuule and Sophie Ransby. Thank you to the department of English and Comparative Literature at Goldsmiths, with special thanks to Maura Dooley and Stephen Knight. Thank you to Judy, Kirat, Molly and Nell. Thank you to all the organisations and publications that have supported by work. Thank you to Niamh. Thank you to Lexia. Thank you to Saz. Everlasting appreciations to the light of Keasa and the team.

Other titles by Out-Spoken Press

sad thing angry • Emma Jeremy

Trust Fall • William Gee

Cane, Corn & Gully • Safiya Kamaria Kinshasa

apricot • Katie O'Pray

Mother of Flip-Flops • Mukahang Limbu

Dog Woman • Helen Quah

Caviar • Sarah Fletcher

Somewhere Something is Burning • Alice Frecknall

flinch & air • Laura Jane Lee

Fetch Your Mother's Heart • lisa luxx

Seder • Adam Kammerling

54 Questions for the Man Who Sold a Shotgun to My Father
Joe Carrick-Varty

Lasagne • Wayne Holloway-Smith

Mutton Rolls • Arji Manuelpillai

Contains Mild Peril • Fran Lock

Epiphaneia • Richard Georges

Stage Invasion: Poetry & the Spoken Word Renaissance
Pete Bearder

Nascent • Vol 1: An Anthology

Ways of Coping • Ollie O'Neill

The Neighbourhood • Hannah Lowe

The Games • Harry Josephine Giles

Songs My Enemy Taught Me • Joelle Taylor

To Sweeten Bitter • Raymond Antrobus

Dogtooth • Fran Lock

How You Might Know Me • Sabrina Mahfouz

Email: press@outspokenldn.com